Wine Time 2

A Coloring Book for Adults

illustrated by
Rachel Jones

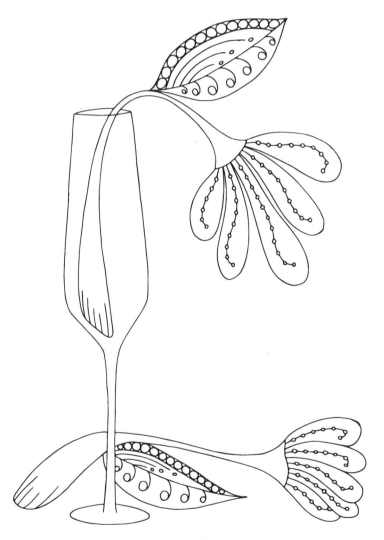

FREE BONUS PAGES

Visit: http://racheljonesarts.com/wine-time-2/ to receive a PDF of 5 bonus coloring pages.

She asked me how I get it all done...

Coffee and wine, sweetheart.

Coffee and wine.

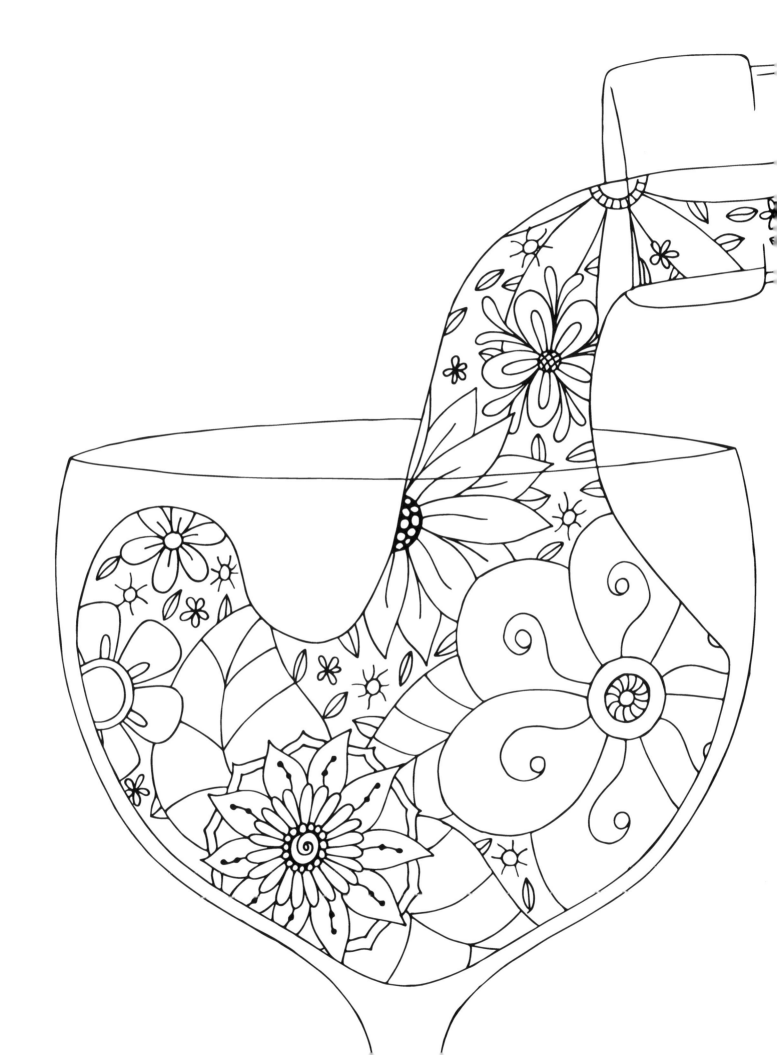

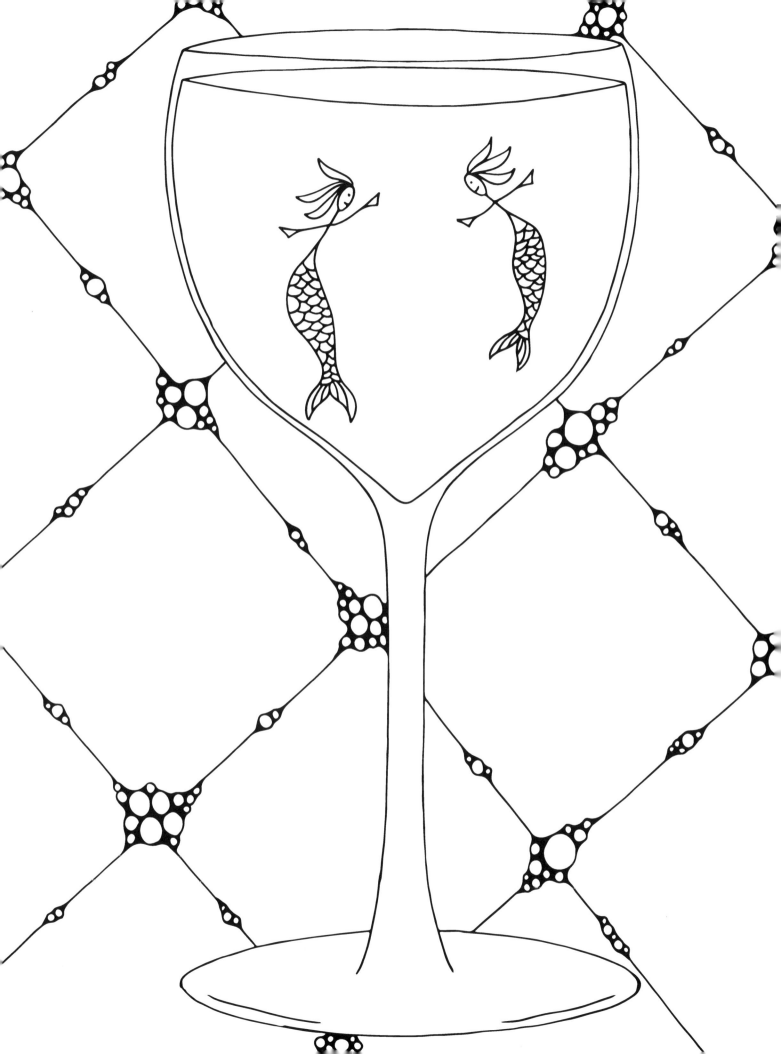

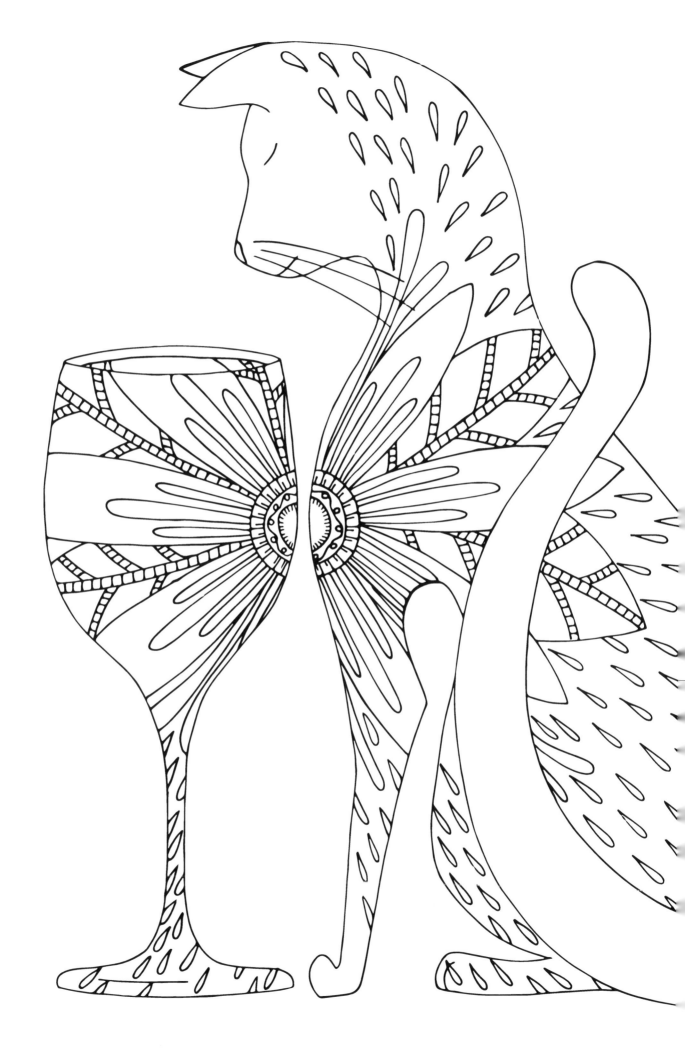

Wine...

because it's not good to keep things bottled up.

Pinot Noir

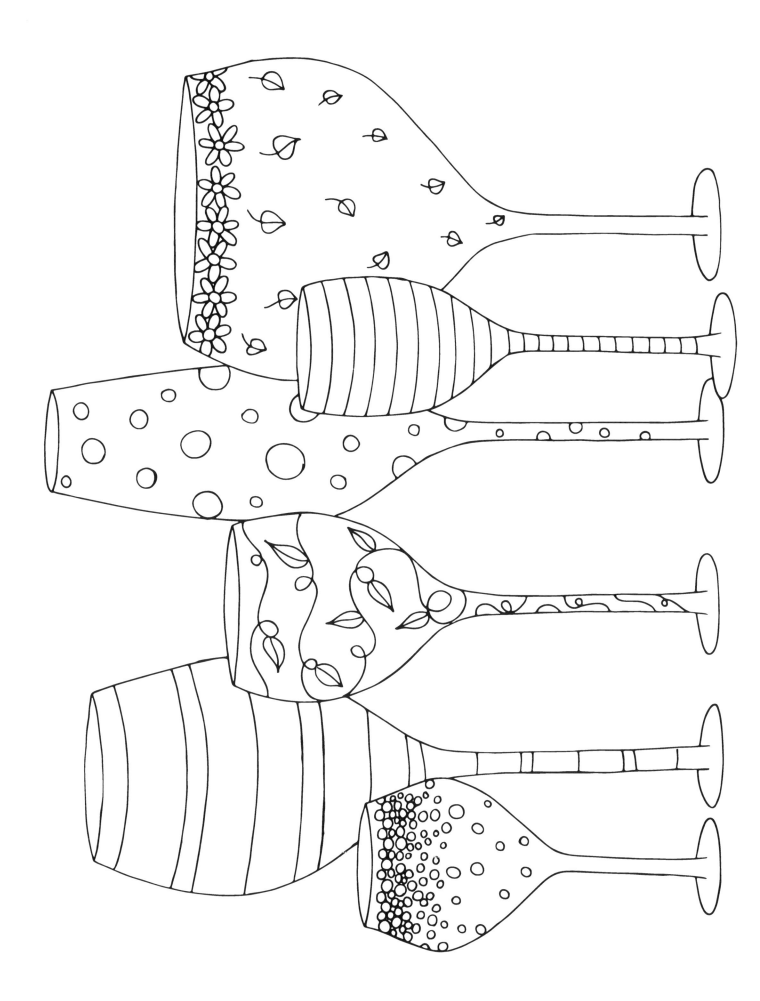

Made in the USA
Lexington, KY
14 March 2017